MW01170733

Leaps of FAITH
My Story of Overcoming FEAR!

By: Lacole Smith

Unaltered Voices Publishing 1765 #440 Baton Rouge, LA 70816

Editors: LaToya Nicole and Latonya L. Brumfield

Formatter: Latonya L. Brumfield

Cover Design: Badrudeen Mikaheel

ISBN 979-8-9857914-1-9

Dedication

I would like to dedicate this book to my mother, the Late Rev. Mother Audrey V. Young. When I think about FAITH I think of my mother. She was a modern-day Job, (Read the story of Job in the bible to learn more about his devoted love for God no matter the test.) Most of my life my mom was dealing with something. One of my strongest memories of her is that her FAITH was unshakeable!

Mom this is from my lips to your heavenly ears!!
Dear my Audrey Marie,

You were always my biggest supporter, my best friend, my rock. It was because of your FAITH that I am able to stand so strong on my own FAITH. You never stopped pushing yourself (even in the midst of pain). Ma, as I take this voyage that God has placed before me, I know that you look down from Heaven each day with a big smile upon your face and pride in your heart. I hope and pray that I make you very proud! Love and miss you so much mom!

-Lacole

Table of Contents

INTRODUCTION

Every day, we go about our lives with a multitude of feelings.
We may experience many fears and may also feel lost, sad,
misguided, depressed, upset, aggravated or alone. This is the
state of mind that the devil wants us in. We do not realize that
the closer we get to God and His word, the more the devil will
attack us. The Bible says in 1 Peter 5:8 (King James Version
[KJV]): "Be sober, be vigilant, because your adversary the
devil, as a roaring lion, walketh about, seeking whom he may
devour." We never want to give the devil that much power
over us. Yes, to some people, this may be easier said than done.

It can be very challenging to pull ourselves out of these low and lonely spots in our lives without seeking some help.

For many of us, going outside of our homes to receive help isn't what we have been taught to do. It was told to many of us, at some point in our lives, that "we don't tell other people our business" or that "you don't have to talk to anyone about what's going on with you; just pray about it, and everything will be okay". However, I have learned that prayer combined with wise counsel has made for lasting results along my journey. Yes, we can trust God by praying for solutions; but we must also trust the solution presented.

Two scriptures that support us seeking help are: Proverbs 11:14 (KJV) "where no counsel is, the people fall, but in the multitude of counselors there is safety" and Proverbs 20:18 (NLT) "Plans succeed through good counsel; don't go to war without wise advice". We need wise counsel. There are areas in our lives in which others may have a better perspective. So, God uses them to guide us to the path of healing. Life can be challenging or just downright brutal. And sometimes it may seem like there is no light at the end of the tunnel. But the Bible says that all things are possible through faith. We all want to live a life so that it is pleasing to God. Daily, we should strive to live like God wants us to live.

When something in our life goes wrong, do we instantly feel like all is lost or like there isn't anything that we can do to fix it? Do we have faith and believe that all will be well because God will bring us through it? I ask you to remove any doubts that you have about your situations and not only lean on God, but also trust that everything will be well. No matter your journey, work to remove your fears and replace them with your faith.

In this book, I will take you through my journey of overcoming fear and tapping into my faith by standing on God's Word. By the power of the word, I overcame obstacles that could have taken my life. During my journey from fear to faith, I grew in prayer, strength, and confidence. At some point, I had to face the person in the mirror and the things I had internalized that hindered my opportunities to move forward.

The hardest part of looking in a mirror is seeing the true 'you'. The mirror reveals those areas we have matured in and those in which we have more work to do. If you see that there is more work to do, embrace it. We grow daily. We all have areas in our lives that we want to change. I had to ask myself: "How can I connect to or help someone else when I have NOT even faced my own fears?" You have to tackle the flaws you see in the mirror. Nobody, and I mean NOBODY, is PERFECT no matter how much we try to be, or, say or think that we are. We all have flaws. Biblical perfection means to mature. Even though we evolve over time and through different journeys, sometimes we still fall short. Therefore, we all need to learn to depend on God! If we don't completely get over ourselves, can we honestly and genuinely say that we are leaning and depending on God?

For years, I heard my parents talk about prayer and faith. They talked about having faith and walking in Faith and even letting faith guide them through life's journeys. As much as I heard these things, you would think that I would have embraced it faster. However, it took me a while to get the concept down. I felt that if I prayed, that was how I exercised faith. I would pray and wish; then I wished and prayed more. Only to realize that something was still missing, and something wasn't connecting. When I did get what I wanted, it didn't seem like I got what I was asked for in the way I was asked for it. When I started to find my faith, I learned that I had to go to him in prayer, have an open heart and mind, and pray unselfishly. I had to be direct about what I asked for, and I had to mix all of that together and pour in the most essential ingredient, FAITH. I had most of the concepts together, and I had everything all in the same place. So, I was ready to use my newfound knowledge the way I needed to use it. Finally, I knew that I had learned the correct way that I needed to pray.

Discovering faith and learning to pray go hand in hand, but let me ask you this simple question: Do you know what faith is? What is it, you ask? Well, Oxford Languages

Dictionary defines faith as, "complete trust or confidence in someone or something." It also is a strong belief in God or the doctrines of a religion, based on spiritual apprehensions rather than proof. The Scriptural definition of faith is the assurance that the things revealed from a promise in the word are accurate, even when unseen, and gives the believer a conviction that what he expects will come to pass. Hebrew 11:1 (KJV) reads, "Now faith is the substance of things hoped for, the evidence of things not seen". The Scriptures encourage us to experiment with our faith. When you start to experiment with your faith, you will find yourself going through new and different journeys in your life. Don't get discouraged but stand firm. Faith isn't something to take lightly, but something to stand on with true belief. Remember that when you pray and ask God for the desires of your heart, exercising faith is to truly believe that he is going to grant them.

Now, in the following chapters, I will share some of my journeys with you. I will explain how my faith was challenged and how God got the glory in the end. Just as I had to go through journeys, some of you will have those same challenges in your life. Your travels may not look like mine, but if you can only keep the faith and stand on the word of God, you will prevail. My prayer is that my transparency will help increase your confidence as you read about the challenges I overcame by Faith. Our journeys may differ, but we were all given enough faith to move mountains, even though it may be as small as a mustard seed. As you move your mountains, pay it forward. because someone is doubting their strength as you read this. May every word in this book encourage you to study your word, speak life over yourself, and be inspired. Some of the roads you have traveled have been heavy, hurtful, and discouraging. And there may have been times that you have even had to cry.

Every tear your cried had a purpose. Yes, it was devastating, and you may have felt all alone. But God was always right there with you. God is always present. Even if we don't see or feel him the way that we think we should, or the way that we would like, he never leaves our side. Most of the time, we are the ones that stray from His presence and His graces.

When I was going through some of my journeys and couldn't talk to anyone, I found comfort in Psalms 23: 1-6 (KJV) which reads:

"The Lord is my shepherd; I shall not want. He makes it me to lie down in green pastures; he leadeth me besides the still waters. He restoreth my soul; he leadeth me in the path of righteousness for his namesakes. Yay, though I walk through the valley of the shadow of death, I will fear no evil; for thou art with me; the role in the staff they comfort me. Thou prepareth a table before me in the presence of mine enemies: how annoyed my head with all; My cup runneth over. Surely goodness and mercy shall follow me all the days of my life: and I will dwell in the House of the Lord forever."

Chapter 1: Faith to Accept Me

"Don't let anyone look down on you because you are young, but set an example for the believers in speech, in conduct, in love, in faith, and in purity."

(1 Timothy 4:12, New International Version [NIV])

I grew up in a small town called Ethel, Louisiana. I went to a very small elementary school. At the tender age of 5, I feared not fitting in. I was still super excited because I would finally get to go to school. I would get to ride on the big yellow school bus that would take all the kids away from the neighborhood each day.

After eating breakfast, we would all line up to go to class for the first day of school. Immediately walking into the classroom, I felt out of place. Can you imagine being five years old and not understanding what or why you felt strange? I felt like I really stood out. It's hard when you're young and don't truly understand why people act differently towards you. Things might have been different for me if I had been around any of the kids before starting school. For a few weeks, I felt like I wasn't supposed to be there. Every day I would go to breakfast and sit with the kids from my neighborhood; we would laugh and have fun. Then, once again, it would be time to get in line to go to class. I remember wishing that someone from my class would come over and talk to me or even be my friend. All the kids from my neighborhood were older than me. After breakfast, they would go to different classrooms.

Our class would go to recess, and the other kids in my class would go one way, and I would find a quiet spot and play alone. I was an only child, so it wasn't hard for me to entertain myself. It would have been even more fun if I had someone to talk to or play with. During that time, I tried to act like it didn't bother me. (Maybe then it didn't) Now that I'm thinking back to that time in my life, I realize that it did bother me. When you must sit, eat, play, and work alone, it is a challenge that I don't wish on anyone.

For weeks, no one would talk to me. And then, one day, a charming girl came over and started talking to me; and, then another one came over. I was thrilled; I didn't want them to know that I was glad they were coming around. This moment was a good turn for a week that would have otherwise been lonely. The next day, more kids started to talk to me; I was so happy that they finally included me in their games, and conversations. I couldn't wait to get home and tell my mother that the kids were talking to me. I had to tell her she was right about saying they would come around eventually.

I wish that I could say that this was the only time in my life that I felt alone or like I didn't fit in, but it wasn't. Even though the kids were starting to come around, I still felt a little out of place. As I began to get older, I thought that this would be something that I wouldn't have to face anymore. Feeling out of place happened more than I expected it to in my life.

However, as I got older, the feeling of being out of place came in different ways. Let me tell you about a few other times I felt like I was out of place in my life. As I look back, I realize that most of the times in which I felt out of place had to deal with something at school.

I started at a new Middle School, adjusted to the new school, and then went to another school shortly after that. I will explain why I had to leave in another chapter. I had to leave all the kids I knew and learned during Middle School to attend a new high school. The only good part about this was that I knew some of the kids because I had participated in middle school with them for a few months.

High school was a challenge because I was different. I didn't look at things the same anymore, and my tolerance was low. I thought I had to have friends to be liked, and now I knew that wasn't true. I could create my destiny.

Many kids go through school feeling like I did; some were even bullied. Most of them won't talk about it or tell someone they need help. I ask that you please pay attention to your kids. I didn't have to deal with being bullied, but I still didn't feel like I was welcomed or accepted by my peers at times.

The good thing about journeys is that you learn from them. We go through different challenges over our lifetime, and each makes us stronger and wiser. We have to know that God controls every event in our lives. He allows us to face whatever obstacle that we have to face. Even feeling out of place, I learned that I was not alone. I knew that I had somebody with me that would always have my back. God is always with us no matter where we are or what we are doing. We must stand up on faith.

All the stories of feeling out of place or feeling like I wasn't accepted were only tests. Each test taught me to hold my own. I had many days when I didn't think that I would be okay or make it to the end of the day, let alone deal with it for a whole school year, but God brought me through it. He allowed total strangers to come to me and make me feel included, as I did belong. We don't always make the first move because we allow the fear of not being accepted or not fitting in to take over, but God will work on your behalf, and you won't know what he's doing. I mean, you would never have a clue that God moved in the way that he did so that the event in your life would happen. Before you know it, things are already done.

The Oxford Languages defines being out of place in many ways, but I will share these two:

- Not in a good situation, not belonging.
- In a setting where one is or feels inappropriate or incongruous.

Now that I'm older and wiser, I wonder if I was feeling out of place because the kids didn't let me in or was I the real problem. Was I in a state of derealization because everything was new and different, and this was my way of protecting myself from the thought of being rejected because I was the new kid? This could be a thought, but I don't believe this was the real reason, but I didn't want to rule this out.

We often want the problem to be someone or something else when, we are part of the problem ourselves. So can you do this for me– take a moment and think about your current situation or a past situation. Are you the reason someone else may be feeling out of place because you had your shield up?

Let's try to be the person that we want others to be toward us. We may be the one that can change someone's life. Never be too afraid of feeling out of place that you can't try to turn things around.

Personal Notes:

_____

_____

_____

_____

_____

_____

_____

_____

_____

_____

_____

_____

When have you felt out of place?

_____

_____

_____

_____

_____

_____

_____

_____

_____

_____

Encouragement scripture:

"The Lord is my strength and my shield; my heart

trusted in him, oh, and I am helped: they are for my

heart greatly rejoiceth, and with my song, I will praise

him." (Psalm 28:7, KJV)

Chapter Two: Faith Tried by Fire

" When you pass through the waters, I will be with you;

And through the rivers, they will not overflow you.

When you walk through the fire, you will not be

scorched, Nor will the flame burn you."

(Isaiah 43:2, New American Standard Bible [NASB])

After having a wonderful summer full of fun and

activities, I was looking forward to going to 7th grade and

starting a new school. I can't say that I wasn't nervous because

I was. It was going to be very different. I had been at the same

elementary school since kindergarten, I was well known with

the students and teachers, but I was still focused on making the change and meeting new people.

I was starting the new school year. It wasn't what I thought it would be; the school was immense, even though it was divided by grade. I was beginning to learn the routine of the new school. I was even making new friends and was thinking about joining a sports team. Then, suddenly, my life would make a drastic change; at least, that's what I felt it was.

I remember that night like it was yesterday. No matter how I try to forget it, it's still in my thoughts. I was washing my clothes to prepare for school the next day. I went to my parent's room, as I did each night before going to bed. My mom was up late that night; maybe she felt something; I guess I'll never know. It is said that your senses are higher when you're pregnant, so perhaps she unknowingly felt something was going to happen.

The next thing I remember was my mom and dad waking me up and telling me I needed to get outside right away. I still didn't know that the house was on fire until I was outside for a few minutes looking at the smoke. I saw my dad go back inside, and all I could think about was that I was about to lose all the new clothes that I had gotten for school. I didn't feel that I was putting myself in any danger. I would go in and be right back out. I had this all played out in my mind. I decided that I was going to go back into the house. Once I was inside, the smoke was so strong. It was burning my eyes and nose, but I was determined to get my clothes out of the dryer. I put my father in jeopardy as well. Because he was the one that came back in to get me out of the house. Through all of this, I still didn't get my clothes.

Once everything settled down, I realized that I had developed another fear of loss. I didn't know those material things could mean so much to me until they were gone. We couldn't save much of our stuff. My oh my! Everything was completely gone. All we had were the clothes on our backs and the few items my dad could pull out of the house before it was destroyed. I felt confused, lost, and hurt; I had no idea what would happen to us next. We didn't have a home anymore. I've heard people say that most people are one event away from becoming homeless; now, I can understand how that could be true.

I had no idea where we would go. We ended up going to my aunt's house to live with her for a few weeks. I felt like everything was going to be okay. I thought that we were going to stay there a while and I would be able to attend the same school, and everything was going to be okay. But I was wrong again. My parents were moving to East Bachar, which meant I would have to change schools.

When I got the news, we would be moving to East Bachar, my heart sank. I would have to learn new people, make new friends, learn a new routine, and ride a bus with people I didn't even know. I thought: "Why was this happening to me? Changes again? Why did I have to move? Why couldn't I stay?" Life felt so unfair. My fear of not fitting in came flooding back like a river. I was finding myself having to face that old fear all over again.

Not only did I have to attend a new school, learn a new neighborhood, ride a new bus, and try to make new friends. And my twin siblings had arrived. Don't get me wrong, I was a little excited to be a big sister, as it helped take my mind off the things that were so mixed up in life.

Things were very different and adjusting was hard for me. I became rebellious, got into trouble at school, and my parents even tried to take me to the detention center. Lord, thank God, they wouldn't allow me to attend!

After that trip, I decided to change how I was acting and pull myself together. Bad decisions would change how I looked at life. The thought of someone telling me when, how, and what I would be doing wasn't who I was or what I wanted to become. I was bigger and better than that, I told my parents I would do better, and I meant what I said. I decided that I would work hard to tackle my fears and try my best to adjust.

Upon returning after that weekend, I wasn't a problem anymore. When I went back to school, I didn't bother my teachers, and my mom didn't have to come regularly to meet with the principal. My grades improved. I even tried to get along with the kids in the neighborhood and school. I attempted to make peace with some of the ones I wasn't that fond of, although they gave me a hard time. I knew that my dad meant business, and I couldn't afford to get into any more trouble anytime soon. I also wanted to start setting my mind straight to be an excellent example for my siblings.

I should have been doing better all along. But like most children that age, I acted up to get attention as it was the only way to articulate how I felt.

I found that I was loved the same even with the additions. However, having to help my mother so much took the fun away from being a child. I didn't have as much fun as the other kids my age, but I learned how to save money, balance a checkbook, comb my hair, take care of my siblings and myself, and a handful of other things that I would have otherwise had to wait to learn later in life.

We may have lost everything in the fire, but we gained so much more. Because of the fire, my life changed. For a long time, I felt the fire took everything from me. Yes, I may have lost a lot that night, but my faith increased. We could have lost our lives as well, but God spared us. I firmly believe everything happens for a reason and has a purpose. We might not know why, but God always knows. We must learn to trust the process.

You may have learned why it had to happen in your life or why you were chosen to be the vessel later in life than I did or from a different event than I. And a lot of times, we do not consider why God uses us, but we all serve a purpose here on earth. I can say one thing, God never puts more on us than we can bear. He already knows that when he assigns you the task that He has chosen for you, you will be able to handle it. You were selected for the mission; the mission did not select you.

Personal Notes:

_____

_____

_____

_____

_____

_____

_____

_____

_____

_____

Have you ever lost anything that meant everything to you?

_____

_____

_____

_____

_____

_____

_____

_____

Encouragement Scripture:

> "God, your God, will restore everything you lost; he'll
>
> have compassion on you; he'll come back and pick up
>
> the pieces from all the places where you were scattered."
>
> (Deuteronomy 30: 3, KJV)

Chapter Three: Faith of a Single Parent

"Strength and dignity are her clothing, and she laughs at the times to come. She opens her mouth with wisdom, and the teaching of kindness is on her tongue." (Proverbs 31:25-26, KJV)

I became a mom at the age of 19. When I found out that I was pregnant, something inside of me instantly shifted to fear. As you can see from my story so far, fear was my go-to reaction. In this situation, I feared not being as good of a parent as my parents had been to me.

I had to understand that God knew I would be a good mother even at that age. I was fresh out of a failed marriage and was back at my parent's house. My beautiful baby girl made the hurt of my marriage seem like it was non-existent. Being a young mother is a challenge; it takes patience. You must be able and willing to give them your love and attention at all times.

I can say that you get tired at times. And it can get overwhelming sometimes. But you must hold steadfast and ensure that your baby is okay. I had to learn how to understand what my baby needed, what would make her happy or upset, and how to be a good parent. Thank God I had the help of my parents during this process!

I don't know how I would have made it without them. When they say it takes a village to raise a child, they are right, it does. And as my daughter grew, I had to lean on my family and even my ex-husband's family as well. It indeed does without a doubt, take a village to raise a child. As I said before, you must be willing to ask for help if you need it. You can't get too caught up in your pride to receive the help you need to ensure that your child is okay.

I'm not going to sit here and act like it was a piece of cake, because it wasn't. Many days I only got a few hours of sleep. Many days I was late for work. And sometimes, I had to call in for work. Once you become a parent, the child's needs come first. It's not about you anymore; it's all about your child or children and what they need.

At the age of 21, I had my twins. This made life even more challenging for me. Imagine parenting two newborns and a 2-year-old; and trying to make everything work while simultaneously trying to keep your sanity. I can tell you the Lord was definitely with me during this process. There were many days that I would say: "Lord, I know that you will not put anything on me that I can't handle".

Having three kids at the age of 21.... In my mind, I honestly didn't think that this was how my life was supposed to be. Sometimes the journey is not what you're ready for, but the journey is one that God is ready for you to travel! Having my twins helped me to grow up. Even though I had an older child, I still wanted to go and do the things that other ladies my age were doing. But once the twins came along, it was time for me to grow up. I started to work overnight to care for them during the day and their dad kept them at night. I remember being tired, overwhelmed and at times feeling completely off balance. I would pray and ask God for the guidance that I desperately needed.

By age 23, I was preparing to have my fourth and final child. I went through a lot during this pregnancy. And by the end of the pregnancy, I knew that this would be the last one. My mind and body had been through so much; I was just plain tired. I'm grateful that I could have her. But the process of getting her here took its toll on my mind and body.

I think at this point, God was trying to tell me that I needed patience, that I needed to slow down, and that I needed to have more focus. When my beautiful baby girl was around six months she was diagnosed with cerebral palsy. In addition to that diagnosis, we were informed that she was hearing impaired. How in the world was I going to be able to manage this in my life?

Eventually, I became a single mother full-time. Their dad would get them every other weekend; and life remained hard. Taking care of four beautiful children mostly on my own was not what I expected for my life.

Now that all my children have grown up, I can look back and say how thankful I am that God allowed me to go through this journey. All my kids are doing great things for themselves. Despite how hard things got for me and despite what I went without having, it was all worth it. To see them turn into the beautiful young ladies that they are now is totally worth every minute of everything that I ever went through! There are many things that I wish I could change, but I wouldn't change having them! Because if I change anything from my past, it will alter my present and/or future. The future that I have is the one that God has prepared for me.

You wouldn't be who you are if you didn't go through the journeys that you went through in the past or that you're going through now. Your life story has already been written; you're just living in the pages of your book. And if everyone is made in God's image, then I will say this— no matter how hard being a single parent may become, always remember that God has your back and that God is always two steps ahead in whatever you're going through. He has already prepared your situation before you even walk into it.

Yes, being a single parent is hard. This is a part of growing up, it's a part of the elevation you need to prepare you for your future. I don't care how young you are when you start the journey of being a mother or a parent, know that everything has its purpose, and that each child is going to take you on a different journey and offer different challenges. In the midst of these challenges and in the midst of these journeys take notes.

I'm so grateful that my Faith in God gave me the ability to push through. If it wasn't for my faith, I don't think I would have been able to achieve everything that I did as a single parent. I had to really lean on and depend on God. I had to pray. And some days I had to cry. But God always came through.

The Bible says:

"And God bless them, and God said unto them, be fruitful, and multiply, and replenish the earth, and subdue it: and have dominion over the fish of the sea, and over the fowl of the air, and over every living thing that moveth upon the Earth." (Genesis 1:28, KJV)

Personal Notes:

_____

_____

_____

_____

_____

_____

_____

_____

_____

_____

_____

How has motherhood changed you?

_____

_____

_____

_____

_____

_____

_____

_____

_____

_____

_____

_____

Encouragement scripture:

> " Her children rise up and bless her; Her husband also, and he praises her, saying: 'Many daughters have done nobly, but you excel them all.'"
>
> (Proverbs 31: 28-29, NASB)

Chapter Four: Faith to Live

"God spared you for a purpose, and the most important thing you can do is to seek that purpose and dedicate your life to it". (Psalm 138:7, KJV)

I've been in a few accidents in the past. With each accident, I could tell that I was starting to get a nervous edge. Whenever I would be in the presence of an 18-wheeler on the highway, I grew anxious. Can you imagine driving around with that type of fear in your mind every single time you get into an automobile or around anything that looks like it might become an accident? You can't even begin to imagine how much of a challenge this was for me. I was always watching my rearview mirror, being that every accident that I had been in involved me being hit from behind.

On March 17th, 2011, I was in an accident that would change my life, my mindset, and my faith. This accident was far from normal. But let me take you back for a moment, because that day started out as a very normal day. Nothing about that day felt strange, looked strange, or even felt different. The kids got off to school just fine and I headed to work. We were getting ready for inventory the next day. Work was going fine; we had to do a little more prepping to get everything right for the next day. Everything about that day was completely normal. Not one thing raised a red flag to indicate that day would change my life forever, even to this very moment.

I received a call from my kids' school saying that the doughnut order was ready for pickup. I told them that I would be there to pick them up as soon as possible because I was at work. They always tell you to follow your first mind, but I was so independent and was always doing things for myself. So, I decided to ask my boss if I could make a quick run to my kid's school to pick up the donuts, drop them off and then head right back to work. She said it would be fine. At least, this was my plan. Again, I say this was my plan, but God had a different plan in store for me that day. He had a plan that I had no idea was brewing.

I called my boyfriend at the time (my husband now Shedric) to tell him that I was going to run to the school. He talked to me on the ride there. Everything was still, as far as I could see, a typical day. I got to the school, picked up the donuts, and talked to my boyfriend for a few more minutes before getting off the phone.

When I was getting ready to make my next which was onto a highway, I noticed that an 18-wheeler was a little way behind me. This is a road that you could really drive fast on if you wanted to, but I wasn't in a real rush. I made the turn onto the highway and remembered the 18-wheeler being behind me, but the 18-wheeler was closer than it had been behind me on the previous highway that we just turned off, with that in mind as I was approaching my turn, I switched on my turn signal. I made sure that I turned it on early because that 18-wheeler was behind me and needed extra time to slow down.

My cousin's car was coming out of the line that I needed to turn into, and another 18-wheeler was coming up the street in the opposite direction. I was sitting still waiting for the 18-wheeler coming from the other direction to pass. I looked up into the rearview mirror and saw that the 18-wheeler behind me was coming toward me faster than it should have been. I was frozen in the thought that it just might hit me. All I could do was whisper a prayer to ask God to please shield me and brace myself for the hit of this truck. At that moment I completely forgot that the other truck was coming from the other direction and still hadn't passed me yet.

The truck hit me. Upon impact of the truck, my seat broke away from the base and I was thrown into the middle of the van. The van started to spin and on about the third or fourth spin my vehicle stopped. I thought it was over and glanced up as the second 18-wheeler hit the front of the van and pushed me back down the street almost to the point at where the accident started. This 18-wheeler took the hood off the van and left the motor lying on the ground. Once everything had finally stopped, I had a calm come over me like I've never felt before. It was like I could feel the presence of God's Grace protecting me and I didn't have any fear in my heart or mind.

My mind came back to the reality of my situation, and I tried to get out because I could smell smoke. I couldn't get out because my seatbelt locked. My cousin, who had seen the whole thing happen right in front of her, sprang into action. Even though she thought the worst had happened and that I was possibly dead because of this horrible accident, she pulled the seat belt up and I slid from under it, then she helped me out of the vehicle.

My back and my hip were in excruciating pain. I was lying on the ground trying to understand the fact that I just had been hit by not just one 18-wheeler, but two of them, and that God had spared my life. As minute as this may seem, considering everything that had happened, I didn't know where one of my shoes was. All I kept hearing in my head was my mother's voice saying that you can't walk around with only one shoe on. Can you imagine something hitting you so hard that it made your shoe come off, and fly out of the vehicle?

My phone that was lying on the passenger seat and my shoe had both been thrown from the automobile and were never found. I asked if someone could please go tell my mother and sister I had been in an accident. I'm still lying on the ground in pain when suddenly, I could hear my sister (Miriam) screaming, and to look at the van I knew she had good reason to think the worst had happened. I was trying to get someone to tell my sister that I was okay. She finally made it to where I was and stayed by me as long as she could.

The ambulance, the police, and my boyfriend all arrived around the same time. At least that's how it seemed to me. I can remember them checking my blood pressure and telling me that it was 120/70. I remember them telling me that I may have had internal bleeding or something going on the inside, because on the outside there weren't any obvious physical cuts or bruises. I had one cut on my pinky finger that came from a small piece of glass while I was getting out of the van.

I was airlifted to Parham Hospital where I underwent many different tests. My sister brought my mother to the hospital, arriving shortly after the helicopter. My dad and brother were there too. A little while later a couple of members from our church arrived at the hospital as well and I remember them praying for me. I sent the message to the school for my kids not to go to practice, but to ride the bus home. I didn't want them to worry so they weren't told what had happened until after they got home.

After all the tests were done, they still didn't find anything wrong, at least not initially. But I was still in a lot of pain. They sent me home. They told me that if the pain continues to come back to the hospital. The following Monday I was still in a lot of pain, so Shed insisted that I go back to the hospital and get more testing. After several hours of testing again, they finally found out that my back had been fractured at L3 and L4. The fracture was coming from both directions, and I was a hairline from causing me to be paralyzed. They put me on bed rest and said if I didn't have to try not to sneeze, bend, fall or make any sudden moves.

Later I had to get a brace for my back and go through more tests. One test revealed an unexpected result that I will discuss in a later chapter. For many years I would have many different procedures done on my back. Life as I knew it was completely different.

I had to learn how to accept help from others. I couldn't do any of the things I did daily. I couldn't help Indea in the same way. She couldn't walk well; so up until then I had to carry her a lot. My heart hurt because I could no longer help her. I couldn't help my mother as I did before either. I would lay in the bed often just thinking, praying, and on some days even crying. Don't get me wrong, I realized just how blessed I truly had been to survive the accident; but still, my faith was shaken.

I know that things could have been so much worse, I could have even lost my life or been crippled. Many people get hit by one 18-wheeler and don't survive, yet here I am complaining about what I could not do instead of focusing on what I could. I knew with all my heart that God kept me here and that I had PURPOSE. But I'm human and I just couldn't see the point of it all. I just couldn't really see what kind of a purpose this could serve at that time.

My fear of accidents began to grow even more intense as time passed. The doctor told me that I could start driving, but I was terrified, so I told most people I couldn't drive yet. I didn't want to seem weak, and this seemed to be my best way around explaining why I wasn't driving. I didn't want people to know I was afraid of something that most people do every single day. This had me trapped in a grave of fear for two years. No, it didn't take me two years to start back driving, but every time an 18-wheeler was near me my anxiety went through the roof.

There were times I was with my kids, and even though I was terrified, I didn't want my children to know the terror that I was experiencing. I always wanted them to see me as a strong single mother, who could handle anything. I wanted them to know that GOD WILL MAKE A WAY no matter what we were going through and that even if life became hard, they would be able to overcome whatever was ahead of them. And, that all they had to do was stay strong and have FAITH in GOD and everything would be fine. They needed to know that life would always work out just how God wanted it too.

I can say this event was definitely the start of my faith increasing exponentially. I had to learn to depend on God to get me through it. Yes, he kept me, that's one thing that I know for sure. This situation taught me that I could ask for help. I also learned that it is okay to need someone to assist you or even do for you what you're not able to do. It doesn't make you WEAK; it makes you HUMAN. Life is an open book full of many different challenges.

God always knows everything. He knows what tasks you will face before you even attempt to go through any of them. When you go to God in prayer, just ask and have faith that you will receive what you ask for. When you pray, you can't say "when you can", or "if you can", but instead, say that you "can and will" with the authority of knowing that the Lord will give you what you ask for. The Bible says, "ask and it shall be given unto you" (Matthew 7:7, KJV). So, if that is what's in the Bible, then why haven't you asked God for what you want. Go to him and ask him to supply you with whatever it is so that your prayer will be. Don't THINK that he will answer but have that amazing faith to know that it is already on the way.

When you are in the midst of things, it may seem like it isn't worth going through, but then you look back and you see that you are much stronger than you ever thought you could be. You can say this because of the test you went through and even the tests that you know you will have to go through in the future. Each test that you endure, whether it's big or small, is something that you can share with others. And I'm sure it will help them as well. Many people walk around hurting and in fear because they feel like they don't have anyone to talk to about their problems. Many people feel like no one can relate to the lemon life has thrown at them. I truly believe that God gives us these tests so that we can share our testimony with others. Your testimony may not be for everyone, but whomever the message is for, they will receive it.

Personal Notes:

_____

_____

_____

_____

_____

_____

_____

_____

_____

_____

What has God brought you out of that you knew you shouldn't
have made it through?

_____

_____

_____

_____

_____

_____

_____

_____

_____

_____

_____

Encouragement scripture:

> "The Lord will keep you from all harm — he will watch
>
> over your life; the Lord will watch over you coming and
>
> going both now and forevermore." (Psalm 121:7-8, NIV)

Chapter Five: Faith to Pick Up the Pieces

" The Lord is near to the brokenhearted and saves those who are crushed in spirit." (Psalm 34:18, NASB)

I was an only child for twelve years. In my younger years, you could always find me around my dad, probably because he was outside a lot and that's where I wanted to be. Around ten I started to hang with my mother more often and was inside a lot more. I didn't and still don't have many friends. I was very close to my mother, she wasn't just my mom, but my best friend, my rock, and my real-life hero. I could talk to her about anything, no matter what it was. For most of my life, my mom dealt with many challenges. She would always tell me to have faith. For as long as I can remember, she talked about God, faith, the power of prayer, and family being very important. Having faith was rooted in me. I couldn't help but have faith. My parents instilled it in me, that prayers could change anything. I only needed to have faith and pray. If it was God's will, then all would be well.

As I got older, I started to understand everything that my parents were talking about. I began to understand that if I had faith and believed, everything would be okay. I began to understand that I should trust the process and know that God is always in control. This gave me the comfort of knowing that everything was going to be just fine. I still knew and understood that it had to be God's will. Everything that happens, must go through Him first.

Even though my mother had been sick, I still had faith that everything would get better and that one day she would be up and back to normal. I believed that God was going to heal her and that all our prayers would be answered. God had answered our prayers, year after year. Even when it didn't seem like she would make it through, she did. My mom was getting better, and we thought life would eventually get back to some kind of normalcy.

One day during our daily talks, it was about two weeks before my mom passed, she asked me a question that surprised me. She asked me if I remember a conversation that we had when I was 12 years old. I said, "I remember", She told me that she and my dad would "help people now" (referring to when I was 12) and I "would help people later". That same day she told me that my "later" had arrived.

The last day that I spent with my mom was different. She seemed to be in so much peace and slept most of the day. When she was awake, we would talk. I always loved talking with my mom. When I left to go home, she was asleep. I told my dad that she seemed to be sleeping so well that I wasn't going to wake her up. I left and went home. I had no idea that would be the last time I would see her alive or hear her voice. I still wish I had woken her up. I never had the opportunity to tell her goodbye.

I remember the phone ringing around 2am that Tuesday morning. That day will always be carved into my thoughts. I thought that they were calling to say my mother was going to the hospital again. I will never forget that call and hearing my sister yell into the phone that my mother was gone– "she's gone!" I jumped up in disbelief. My heart felt like it had been pulled from my chest. In that moment I felt lost, hurt, upset, heartbroken, and disappointed. The day my mother closed her eyes, I think a part of me died with her as well. I had all these emotions hitting me all at one time. Those emotions hit me like a wave out on the ocean as it crashed into the ocean water below it. I fought to stop crying, yet I couldn't stop, each breath I took seemed to be harder than the one before it. Each step I made felt so heavy and painful. I couldn't believe that my faith and prayers didn't keep my mom here with us. I wasn't ready for her to be gone!

The ride to my parents' house was the longest ride I had ever taken. When I got there, all I wanted to do was bring her back. She looked like she was just sleeping peacefully. I wanted her to say something, to let me know that she was okay, that everything was going to be alright, and this was not real. The reality of it all was that she was gone. She wasn't coming back. And I would have to live the rest of my life without my mother or my best friend. I felt like my prayers were unanswered. And in that very moment, my faith was shattered.

Nothing can make it more clear to you that your loved one is gone than to witness the moment that they are loaded into the coroner or funeral van. At 6:00 a.m. that morning, I witnessed my mother being put into the back of the funeral van. I had seen my mother being loaded into an ambulance on many different occasions, but that feeling is not close at all to what I felt at that moment. That was another blow, unless you've been through this, you probably wouldn't understand. To know that she would never come back home again was too much for me to handle.

The days before the funeral seemed like a blur. I knew that we had to plan and prepare to lay my dad's wife, and our mother to rest. But I was just numb and going through the motions of getting everything done. This was so hard and the whole process was just mentally draining and emotionally challenging. We had to push ourselves. We had to get the programs together, get the time of the service, the church, and do all the other tasks that needed to be completed to have our mother's service.

The day finally came that we would lay my mother to rest. I don't remember much, but I remember that my heart hurt, and I longed to have my mother back here and alive. This is a pain that I can't begin to explain. I felt lost and confused. I felt like God had betrayed us. My faith was shattered like a mirror hitting the floor, and I knew it would take strength to pick up the pieces.

Once the funeral and repass is over and you go back home knowing that this was really the last time you will see your loved one, it all hits you like a ton of bricks. You really start to feel alone. The calls and text messages slow down and eventually stop. The visits come to a halt. While everyone around you is going back to their normal routine, you are still trying to process everything. Your mind is twirling, your heart hurts, the tears keep falling, and sometimes you have no clue why you're crying. It can be hard to get out of bed and face this new version of life. Your feelings are everywhere.

My mother would always say that God would see you through, just have Faith, don't let the devil take control. I could hear this clearly in my head. That didn't stop the sting of betrayal from being all I saw at that moment. In that moment and for the next few years that is all I felt. With each day that passed my faith was decreasing. I started to think, how could my mother say these things, and yet God took her from us. The main things that I remember hearing went out the window. I didn't want to have faith, I didn't want to hear what she had said time after time, I just wanted to be angry and bitter. I thought: "Why didn't God see me through?". The devil was making me doubt the word of God.

We go through life turning God off and on like a faucet. We normally call on him when we need something, when we feel like it, when we are in trouble, and when we want something fixed that we probably messed up to start with. No matter what we do, no matter how much we turn Him off and how dusty our faith in God gets from being set aside and placing Him on the shelf, he is always by our side and continues to love us just the same. It's amazing how much God really loves us. All he wants us to do is have faith in His word. If we took the time to love God as he does us, the world would look totally different.

Personal Note:

_____

_____

_____

_____

_____

_____

_____

_____

_____

_____

Do you have a time when your Faith was challenged?

_____

_____

_____

_____

_____

_____

_____

_____

_____

_____

Encouragement Scripture:

> "Therefore you too have grief now, but I will see you
>
> again, and your heart will rejoice, and no one will take
>
> your joy away from you." (John 16:2, NASB)

Six: Faith to Rebuild

"He replied, 'You of little faith, why are you so afraid?'

Then he got up and rebuked the winds and the waves,

and it was completely calm". (Matthew 8:26, NIV)

I remember August 12, 2016. The morning started out strange. I remember getting up and watching tv. For some reason, the dogs were cutting up in the backyard. I guess they could feel that something was about to happen.

It started raining and the water in the backyard where one of the dogs was kept began to rise. One of the twins went and moved her near the back patio. The other twin moved the other dog into a room at the back of the house. I went to move their car under the garage since the water was getting a bit high. We had done it before, we didn't have a reason to think that this time would be different.

Once we finished, we came inside to change clothes. I looked at the news report on the tv, and I didn't get to hear what all they had to say because the water started coming in through the sliding doors in the living room. We got some towels to get the water up. Yet I still wasn't worried that we would flood because the water wasn't much higher than before. The rain had stopped, so I was sure everything would be ok.

I called my fiancé and told him that the water was still rising, but I still thought that we would be ok. Only a few minutes had passed when I called him back to say we couldn't get my truck out of the driveway because the water was too high. He said that he would go get my youngest daughter and head that way. We started putting everything up high in the house and trying to get a few things to take with us just in case we couldn't return to the house that day.

A few of the neighbors were leaving out in their boat. Some of the neighbors said they would try going to the upper level of their homes. I just couldn't believe that the water was still rising, and it was only sprinkling. When my fiancé arrived, we had water up to our waist. The water had all kinds of stuff in it. I had never seen so many spiders as I saw walking through that water. I was hoping we didn't come across any snakes because we didn't have anything to help us.

For a lot of Louisiana residents, they had never known this challenge. The flood of 2016 was a Flood for the history books. It had been over 100 years since a flood of this magnitude had happened. Some homes were completely under water.

In the days after the flood, we would go and see if we could get back to the house every day, it wasn't until day 4 that we could get to the house and go inside. The road leading to our home was still flooded. The only way we would have been able to get to the house would have been in a boat. The house took on at the least 4 feet of water. It was by the grace of God that the automobiles we had to leave in the garage were fine. I know it was nothing but God answering my prayers. I prayed so much that our automobiles would be ok, and he answered my prayers. The house on the other hand was going to need lots of work to be able to live in it again.

We started to gut the house and found out that the house had flooded before, had mold that was there from a previous flood, and had even had a small fire. The following week my fiancé ended up in the hospital for 2 weeks with a staph infection in his leg from being in the dirty floodwaters. Due to his hospitalization, he missed my daughter's wedding. But once he was out of the hospital, we decided to cut our ties with the house and move on. We lived at my dad's house for a while before moving into an apartment.

During the flood, we lost almost everything. Many things we lost can't ever be replaced. This was a hard blow, not just to my faith, but to my mental health as well. I kept wondering why this was happening to us and why I couldn't catch a break. It was just too much to deal with.

The flood had taken another chunk out of my faith. I felt like God wasn't listening to me. I had just lost my mom a few months before, and now this. I wondered why God was doing this to me and my family. I was so broken, I felt so lost.

Normally, I could talk to my mom, but that option was gone too. What would I do, how in the world was I going to get past this hurt in my heart? I even stopped praying for a little while. I felt like it couldn't get any worse than this.

Life itself didn't get worse, but my mental, emotional, and I guess you can even say my spiritual health, had taken a blow. I was becoming someone I didn't even know anymore. Everything made me upset or got under my skin. I wasn't happy and even when I should be smiling, I found a reason to be unhappy. Who was this person in the mirror? I didn't have a clue who I was, so how was anyone else going to know? Through all of this, I still had some faith, but it was hanging on by a thread. Unfortunately for me

When you feel like you're at your lowest low, and nothing is going how you thought it would go, have faith in God. In the midst of everything, I had to believe that God would bring me and my family through this. I also believed that he would never let me go through anything that I couldn't handle. Everything you are going through is to help take you to the next level. It's setting you up for your testimony, and through that, you will be able to help someone else. I dare you to just try him for yourself, he will never fail you. You can and will, make it through whatever you are dealing with. God will always be there for you.

Personal Note:

_____

_____

_____

_____

_____

_____

_____

_____

_____

_____

Have you ever had to deal with a flood? This could be water or life challenges that just kept coming.

_____

_____

_____

_____

_____

_____

_____

_____

_____

_____

Encouragement scripture:

> "Fear thou not; for I am with thee: be not dismayed; for I am thy God: I will strengthen thee; yea, I will help thee; yea, I will uphold thee with the right hand of my righteousness." (Isaiah 41:10, KJV)

Chapter Seven: Faith to Flee Depressions Pit

"These things I have spoken unto you, that in me ye might have peace. In the world ye shall have tribulation: but be of good cheer; I have overcome the world".

(John 16:33, KJV)

Many people go through life and get really good at hiding things from their friends, family, and even co-workers. On the outside, everyone would think that things are just fine and that your life is going well. People around you, most of the time, don't even see the signs that are right in front of them. When you have seen the signs, or thought that someone you know was dealing with depression, did you try to get them some help?

I know firsthand that when you are dealing with depression, you must get to the bottom of what's going on. This can be done by being open with yourself first, and then with the people around you. Most people won't ask for help. I know this to be true because I went years doing my best to hide my depression from everyone around me.

I battled with depression for three years. To the outside world and probably to most of my family and friends, everything was "normal"; they didn't even have a clue that I was dealing with depression. I learned to work hard to hide the fact that anything was wrong with me. Looking back, I can't even say what specific event sent me spiraling into the depression that I would carry with me for years. I will say, however, that I was hit with many obstacles in a small period of time. I remember walking around and trying to smile, act, and feel like nothing was wrong with me. Sometimes I didn't know what was worse, trying to hide it from everyone or the depression itself. It was consuming me. And, it was slowly destroying the faith that I had left. I was so low that I almost didn't think that I would even come back from the pit I had fallen into.

I would go to work and church and smile around everyone, but once I was back home in my room I would cry, think of ways that I could hurt myself or those around me, or even just drink alcohol till I fell asleep. Each day it got harder and harder to even get out of bed, get dressed, and go about my daily duties. I just wanted to find the darkest spot I could and hide there forever.

My attitude was different, my patience was thin, and my heart was heavy. I had lost so much in 2016 that I truly didn't think I knew how to be happy anymore. Honestly, I didn't think that I deserved to be happy. It seemed like every time anything good happened in my life, it only brought something horrible afterward. At that time, I really didn't care when I would hurt someone's feelings or if I made them upset. Because I thought that if they got mad or felt hurt, that maybe they could understand how I was feeling inside.

Losing my mom took a big part of my happiness, then the flood came and took even more. It didn't stop there. I would face more losses before the end of 2016. I just couldn't figure out how to come to grips with everything that was happening in my life or even why I had to deal with it all. I didn't think anyone would even understand and that no one would care. Life was a blur, and my faith was completely shattered. I felt like God had let me down. I felt like he took me out to a clothesline and left me hanging out to dry.

Despite everything 2016 threw my way, I still got married, my first granddaughter was born, and my oldest daughter got married also. Still, these happy moments weren't enough to help me. This pit of depression was deep. The deeper it became the harder I had to work at hiding it from everyone.

I kept to myself a lot. I was sneaking around just to drink. And my attitude was horrible. I didn't realize how bad things were. You can't fix a problem if you don't know that you have one or admit that you have one. Honestly, at that moment

I didn't think I had a problem. I excused myself because I thought that this was my way of coping.

I can't recall how I ended up at the doctor's office with my grandson, but what I do remember is that this was the day that I realized that I had a problem. I was sitting in the lobby, and I picked up one of the magazines to read while we waited to see the doctor. As I flipped through the magazine, I saw an article about the signs and symptoms of depression. I read the whole article. And after reading it, I knew that I was dealing with some form of depression. Most people don't know what to look for, and symptoms may vary from person to person. Here are a few symptoms that I personally experienced:

- Loss of sleep
- Loss of appetite
- Short Temper
- Drinking and trying to hide it
- Lack of interest
- Low will to get out of bed
- Wanting to be alone

- Change in attitude

The wheels in my mind started turning. I thought to myself: "I know something is off, but I know that this can't be me. I'm too strong of a person to be dealing with depression. I don't let things get to me like this". Time passed and I kept seeing that article in my mind. I couldn't shake the fact that I really could be dealing with depression. The hardest part of having depression is admitting to yourself that you are depressed.

Now that I'm aware of the fact that I was suffering from depression, I had to do a few things to get myself out of this ditch. I thought I could do it by myself. But if I did, would I truly be free? First, I decided that I needed to start praying more and that I should ask God for guidance to do the right thing. If I would have prayed more often, leaned not on my own understanding (Proverbs 3:5, KJV), and let God have full control, I'm sure things would have been a lot different. Next, I had to admit to myself that I really had a problem that was out of my control. Many times, we think that we know what's best for us. This is so far from the truth. God has the key to answering any problem we have. Trusting the process. I scheduled a session with a psychologist. While in therapy, I learned that I was still grieving. I never allowed myself to truly deal with losing my mother. I thought that if I didn't talk about it or think about it, I would be fine. That was far from the truth.

I needed to learn to love myself again and take better care of myself. How could I pour into anyone from an empty cup? I felt like I was abandoning myself. I had to fix this, not just for myself, but for the sake of my kids as well. I had to do something. I needed to make a change. I put this list into play:

- Prayer: We often hear that prayer changes things, that is so true. I made it a point to pray 3 times per day. My prayer was specific. I was determined to beat this feeling inside of me that was running my life.

- Faith: I had to lean on the faith that I had to guide my path. It doesn't matter how much you have if you have it and use it.

- Strength: I had to renew the strength that I had. I had to believe that I would be able to turn this situation around. I'm not going to say that it is easy, but it is worth it.

- Self-Love: I had to learn to love myself again. When I say that I'm not talking about how you look in a mirror, but how you look on the inside. That confidence that makes you step higher, smile brighter and dream a little bigger.

- Therapy: I also made it a priority to go get some help. I talked to a psychologist to help me navigate everything that I was dealing with. We can talk with our friends and family, but sometimes you must dig a lot deeper to heal properly.

Once I put all these into motion, I began to slowly dig myself out of that pit of depression. It didn't happen overnight. It took a lot of work, I had to change my way of thinking, and I had to allow myself to grieve as well. The process was lengthy, but it did happen. Prayer, faith, strength, self-love, and therapy were the steps on the ladder I used to climb out of that Depression Pit!

Life has the tendency to throw you lemons, and there will be times that it's more than you think you can handle at one time. If you take all those lemons, put them together, and make yourself some lemonade, you will see that something sweet can come from all that bitterness. That even something so tart can change into something you want to hold onto is amazing. You don't want life challenges to turn you into someone who's bitter, cold-hearted, or evil. You must give it to God and trust him to make it right. Then, let it go. If you don't it will weigh you down.

I can tell you this because that's what happened to me. I went around for years with this jacked-up attitude, hatred in my heart, and a bitter spirit, all because I allowed life (lemons) circumstances to turn me into someone I didn't even know anymore. That was not the person I wanted to be or continue to be. I had to realize that to get better, I had to relinquish all my thoughts and feelings to God and give him control over my life again. My renewed faith in God helped me with this process. Was this process easy? No, not at all. I had days that I just wanted to go back to my old ways, that is what the devil wants us to do. We must keep praying, keep the faith and keep pushing. God will definitely see us through.

Personal Note:

_____

_____

_____

_____

_____

_____

_____

_____

_____

_____

Have you ever dealt with Depression and how did it affect your life?

_____

_____

_____

_____

_____

_____

_____

_____

_____

_____

_____

Encouragement scripture:

"Peace I leave with you, my peace I give unto you: not as the world giveth, give I unto you. Let not your heart be troubled, neither let it be afraid". (John 14:27, KJV)

Chapter Eight: Faith to Remain Whole

"Nevertheless, I will bring health and healing to it; I will heal my people and will let them enjoy abundant peace and security."

(Jeremiah 33:6, New Living Translation [NLT])

I prayed: "Lord, here I am again, I know that this too is only a test. I truly need your guidance and strength to continue to be the person you want me to be. Lead me in the direction in which you want me to go. I know I was sent this test to be a guide and blessing to help someone else during their time of trial."

For 2020, I knew I needed to go to the doctor for my regular checkups, but I was always so busy. Work, other things, and the Covid pandemic came as my excuse to not go and have my health checks. In my mind, if I wasn't dealing with any pain, sickness, or discomfort everything was just fine. I thought it didn't matter what the doctor said about making sure that I came in every 6 months to get checked. I thought that surely, I could miss one year if I wanted to, it wouldn't do any harm. That's what I thought anyway.

If you are walking around with this attitude, let me tell you to change that real quick. All this year I've been dealing with one thing or another. This has been all because I missed going to the Dr. to follow up as I was supposed to. Take the time and go to your doctor, your health is very important. It will save you a lot of time and money.

Let me tell you about this life challenge I've been faced with. I went to have my Mammogram done in February. A few days later, I got a phone call asking me to come in to have an ultrasound of my breast done because they saw something abnormal. They also said there was no need to be alarmed and that this sort of thing happens sometimes and that it by no means meant that they would find anything. I went into prayer, and I set the ultrasound appointment. I remember praying and waiting for them to return to the room. I already had a feeling deep down that I would have to come back for more tests or something. It was just the way the tech kept looking at the screen and kept going to the same area. Finally, they came back in and said that they saw a spot that was about 5 mm and that they would like to see if the doctor wanted to set up a biopsy. Again, I went into prayer. I had been down this road before in 2011, and I was very calm at that moment. I wasn't worried because I believed that it would be fine.

I arrived to have my biopsy done and I was calm and at peace, they did all the prep and the tech walked me through how the biopsy was going to be done, now all I had to do was wait. They called me into the room to perform the procedure. It seemed to be simple enough, yet I was a little afraid of what would happen. I know that they were going over everything with me again on what was about to happen, but I had gone into prayer that everything would go well and that it would come back fine, and I wouldn't have to deal with any of this again. I answered the Radiologist, but I was rooted into my prayer. I didn't hear anything he said. I had my biopsy, they informed me that it would be 5-7 days for the results to come back and that the doctor would call me. I left feeling good about everything. All I had left to do was pray and wait.

The wait ended up being about 9 days, by that time my nerves were getting the best of me. I was beginning to have doubts. My mind was all over the place, with all kinds of thoughts. I was wondering if it really was cancer and how bad it might have been. I wondered if I would have to have my breast removed, etc.

The first time my doctor called I was at work and missed the call. I called back once I saw that he had called, and he had left the office and would be back the next day. Early the following day he called me again. I couldn't believe I missed the call again. I had an appointment for a post-op the next day so I said to myself if I don't talk with him today at least he will go over everything tomorrow. That's exactly what happened.

I went to my appointment with my nerves high. I was so worried about what he would say. I waited in the room hoping that the news wasn't as bad as I was letting my mind think it was. That he would have great news, and everything would be back to normal. That's not what happened but thank God it wasn't worse.

He started off by saying that the biopsy came back benign, but my chances of getting breast cancer was high and he wanted me to go see an oncologist. I was glad to hear that it was benign, but lord I was nervous to hear what the oncologist would say. I left my appointment with mixed emotions. I didn't know if I wanted to cry or shout for joy. I went to see the doctor wanting him to say that everything was benign, and I could just continue my 6-month process as usual.

I truly didn't know how to react to going to see the oncologist. The day of my appointment arrived, and I felt lost. I just knew I would get some bad news. I was sitting in the lobby waiting to be called back and my nerves were very high. The nurse came to call me back, as I was sitting in the exam room I went into prayer. I had to pray to keep my nerves calm and I know that if anyone could fix this it would be Jesus.

The doctor came in and she was explaining everything to me. Some of the stuff was easy to understand and others were more complex. When I didn't fully understand something, she broke it down for me.

When I left, I felt a little better but was still overwhelmed about having to start a chemo pill. Some people hear the word chemo and think the worst. But when I say that this was all for a reason, I know that God got me and my situation. I'm human, I still had to process everything. I had to give myself time to process it all.

My thoughts were up some days and down on other days. Here we go again, I wondered why I was facing another challenge. I prayed "Lord, it seems like the more I try to get my life in order the more the devil tries to test my faith. I refuse to let the devil steal my joy. Lord, I know if you brought me through everything else, you will bring me through this as well." I've been on my meds for a little while now, and everything is going well. I make sure I do what the doctor asks me to do. And I get checked every six months to stay on top of my status. I don't have cancer. The chemo pills are used as a preventative to help keep my levels down so that I may be able to avoid getting breast cancer.

I know when people hear the words cancer or chemo, their minds automatically think the worst. If you would just take your faith to another level, change your diet, and change your mindset, you will be so amazed at the things that you can accomplish. I wake up each morning giving thanks to God for being in charge of my life and situation. I have faith that everything is going to be wonderful, and I can handle this. I'm still in the midst of this challenge, but my FAITH is strong, and I know God got me.

You must take ownership of your situation. You can take ownership of any situation in your life by having a little faith, it doesn't take much. Don't let it control your life or how you think. I know some of you may be dealing with cancer, headaches, heartaches, drug addiction, alcohol addiction, depression, stress, worrying, eating disorders, and strokes; and the list could go on and on. Can you do just this one thing for me? Go into a quiet spot, close the door, turn off the lights, close your eyes, take a deep breath, and say a prayer. It may be long or short, it may just be you taking the time to tell God what is going on or what's on your mind. Whatever you do, take the time to expand your faith, your relationship, and your prayer time with God. Make this part of your daily routine. You will start seeing the difference and you will be grateful for making this simple change to your lifestyle.

Personal Note:

_____

_____

_____

_____

_____

_____

_____

_____

_____

_____

_____

What are you dealing with that poses a challenge in your life?

_____

_____

_____

_____

_____

_____

_____

_____

_____

Encouragement scripture:

"The Lord is my strength and my shield; My heart trusts in Him, and I am helped; Therefore, my heart triumphs, and with my song I shall thank Him. (Psalm 28:7, NASB)

Chapter Nine: Faith During a Pandemic

"so that your faith might not rest on human wisdom,

but on God's power." (1 Corinthians 2:5, NIV)

It was the year 2020. If we look at the world around us now, so much is going on. Many people are facing things that they have never seen or heard of before. Many have lost sight of what faith truly is and how to tap into it.

Depending on the bible version you may read the word faith appears anywhere from 336 - 521 times. Think about it, if the word faith appears these many times, there's a reason and it must be of importance.

I remember the first time I heard anything about COVID, I had no clue what it was or what it would be capable of doing. My mind went from being excited that we would have a few days off from work to having a major fear of the unknown. I would sit in the house watching the news every day for hours worried about someone in my house or one of my family members getting sick from this virus. When a lot of people started dying, it became so much harder for me. I was scared to go to the store to get the items we needed. I didn't want anyone coming over to visit. I was trapped in my own world of fears. Life as we knew it had changed, and anyone that knows me knows that I wasn't good with change. I liked things to go with the flow. I needed things that I'm familiar with. The current state of the world was not something I was familiar with.

The first month was horrible. I was afraid all the time. But I didn't want anyone to know this, I wanted them to think I was strong and positive that we would get through this just fine.

By month 2, I was still afraid, but it wasn't as bad. I still didn't like going out much, but I would make trips to the store at least once a week. If I had to go more than once I would try to get there when they first opened because there weren't many people out.

By May they were saying we would be headed back to work and my fears all came flooding back. I questioned the logic of the decision to go back to work. Do they not understand that COVID was killing people and we were expected to go back out there in it.

The closer May 15th got, the more afraid I became. How will this work? How can I run a store with people wanting to try on clothing? I know that this is going to be a challenge that we are not ready to face. People were not taking this pandemic seriously and that terrified me. I called on the Lord, "Help me. I need you to take control of my fears and to give me strength. I need to go out into this world of the unknown. Lord, I pray that I will not have any problem, and all will go well. I ask that you put a shield of protection around this business and each

employee that must come back to this work environment."
This was my prayer daily.

I know that there will be times in your life when you don't know which way to turn. You may feel used, unappreciated, or even lost at times, but I know a Man that listens to all our problems and guides us. Keep the faith, and if you don't have any, I encourage you to build it. The God I serve is always on time. He may not come at that moment you want Him to, but He always shows up.

No matter what we are up against, God will see you through. He is never short of his word. We must understand that sometimes we need to take the first step. We shouldn't always feel like God has to do everything while we sit back and collect the fruit of the harvest God has planted for us.

We all are children of a King, that makes each of us a prince or princess. We were born into riches from God, but you must earn them. You earn your riches by having unshakeable faith in your Father. Doing what is right even when you don't want to or don't feel like you need to. Telling others about how great God is and how if you just have faith the size of a mustard seed, you can accomplish great things. Faith and prayer can take you places you never thought you would be able to go and allow you to see things you never thought you could see. You only must believe, and your faith will do the rest.

I have been through many different trials in my lifetime. In some I had no clue how I would make it through. I haven't always had the faith that I have now. It took many years to get myself to this point, where I know that if I have the faith and pray for the things, I want to accomplish in life I could. My faith has taken me to a different level in my life. It took me to a place where I knew that I would make it.

Faith is a key that can unlock doors and move mountains if you keep pushing and praying. I encourage you to close the grave on your fears and allow faith to be born.

Personal Notes:

_____

_____

_____

_____

_____

_____

_____

_____

_____

_____

_____

How strong is your faith?

_____

_____

_____

_____

_____

_____

_____

_____

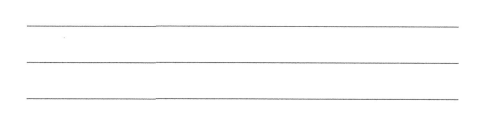

Encouragement scripture:

> "But without faith it is impossible to please him: for he that cometh to God must believe that he is, and that he is a rewarder of them that diligently seek him."
>
> (Hebrew 11:6, KJV)

Chapter Ten: Conquering Fear with Faith

"For God hath not given us the spirit of fear; but of power, and of love, and of a sound mind."

(2 Timothy 1:7, KJV)

Are you walking around in FEAR? Have you ever said to yourself why am I going through so many trials in my life? What have I done to deserve all of this? Why is it that when I think I'm just about to make it to the top of these mountains I get knocked right back down? I have asked myself a few of these questions in my lifetime.

Fear comes to us in so many forms, and most of the time we don't even know that we have been conquered by fear.

Fear is a sneaky little thing, it creeps up on you slowly, next thing you know, it has taken a toll on your life. It has you at a point where you make decisions that you probably wouldn't otherwise make. Many people underestimate the power that fear can have over their lives.

If we investigate the definition of the word fear, it's defined in the Oxford Languages as "an unpleasant emotion caused by the belief that someone or something is dangerous, likely to cause pain or a threat. Also, to be afraid of (someone or something) likely to be dangerous, painful, or threatening."

Your emotions can change your thought to believe that something or someone is out to get you or want to harm you. Yes, in some cases the idea that you have about something is true, and you have the right to be concerned about something that has your curiosity up. There are times that these thoughts or concerns couldn't be further from the truth. Now you have allowed your mind to create a level of fear. It can take you to places that some never make it back from. There are many different things that can cause fear in someone's life, I will list some, and if it is something you are dealing with in your life, I encourage you to have faith to know that it can get better. Here are more examples of things that you might even think about using your faith to conquer.

- Fear of flying
- Fear of dying or losing a loved one
- Fear of heights
- Fear of the dark
- Fear of being alone
- Fear of snakes or lizards
- Fear of spiders, bugs, etc.
- Fear of an elevator, stairs, or escalators
- Fear of fire
- Fear of doctors or nurses
- Fear of needles, etc.

These are just a few things. But with each of these, I know, if you have the faith to believe, that you can be cured of these fears. It is possible. I can say this with great confidence because I had a fear of flying years ago. I didn't want anything to do with a plane. If I was driving and a plane passed over the road, I was afraid. I was afraid of going to the airport to pick someone up. Why did I have this fear? It was most likely from watching some horror movie. I felt like I would be on the plane in a storm, and it would crash on some highway or something.

God can move these fears from your mind and heart and turn this around for you. He did that for me. I had a little help. But I know it was God's way of removing this fear from me. Let me tell you a little bit of this story. Two of my friends and I were going to New York, a month before the trip one of my friends told me they were about to pay for the stuff we needed for this trip. All the time I thought we would be driving to this destination. They told me 5 days before leaving that we would be going via airplane. I didn't want them to know how scared I was. I called my doctor to get some anti-anxiety pills to help keep me calm to get through this.

The day arrived and we made it to the airport. My heart felt like it was going to jump right out of my chest. The walls looked like they were closing in on me. Everything about the airport felt like a horrible dream that I couldn't wake up from. We went through all the bells and whistles: check in, security check, boarding wait area. They called our flight to board the plane. I had my meds from the doctor. in hand ready to take the moment we took off. I don't even know how I made it to my seat. All of that was just a blur to me. I remember my friend asking me if I wanted to sit by the window or on the end. I don't even know what my reply was. All my focus was on the plane and the thought that it was going to take off.

This might seem strange, but I could hear my heart beating in my chest. I did my best to seem like I was okay, but God knows I was far from that. The plane started down the runway to proceed to take off. I whispered a prayer to God and said that I didn't want to feel like this. I wanted to take this flight without taking this medicine. I prayed: "Please get us to our destination without any harm or danger coming to any of us." I guess my prayer worked. I didn't have to take the medicine. But my fear wasn't completely gone yet. I could say that flying wasn't as bad as I thought it was though.

When it was time to return home, we made it to the airport and then to our boarding area. While waiting there one of my friends received a call. She received some bad news.

From that point we went into fix it mode to make sure she was okay and to get her where she needed to be. Pattie and I got on the plane to head to our next airport. And from there, we would catch another flight to make it home. The flight didn't even matter anymore. The love for my friend and what she was going through was more important than any fear I was holding on to.

We made it to the next airport for our final flight home. We boarded the flight, and the weather was very bad. So, we had to sit on the runway for nearly an hour before taking off. I used that time to pray and ask God to please remove this fear that I had of flying. Lord knows sitting on a plane in the middle of a storm wasn't the answer. As my prayer came to an end the rain did as well. The airplane started to take off.

I had a window seat on this flight and as the plane began to rise, I could feel my fears starting to return. I closed my eyes and began to pray. This time my prayer was different. I asked God to please step in and take this fear from my heart. The ride was a little bumpy, this type of ride was basically my biggest fear. The rain was coming down, but the more turbulence we hit, the more I started to calm down. I guess God allowed me to come face to face with my fear to start getting over it. Once we landed, I was at peace with flying. We had made it safely to our destination even in the midst of a storm.

God never desired for us to live in fear, but to live a life of happiness and prosperity. He wanted us to live a life of peace and happiness. Yes, this might not have played out as planned, because of Adam and Eve. But God still wants the same thing for us today. We must have the faith to believe in his promise. God has never fallen short of his word.

Even when we must deal with our inner fears, we have to make the decision to lean and depend on God. We must know that he will see us through whatever it is that we are going through.

Personal Note:

_____

_____

_____

_____

_____

_____

_____

_____

_____

_____

_____

Do you have a fear that you haven't Conquered yet?

_____

_____

_____

_____

_____

_____

_____

_____

_____ _____

_____ _____

_____ _____

Encouragement Scripture:

"Cast all your anxiety on him because he cares for you."

(1 Peter 5:7, NIV)

Acknowledgements

I would like to acknowledge and thank my husband and children who without their love and significant support, this book may not have come to pass. Additionally, there are a host of other family members and friends who were very supportive in the journey of writing my first book and for them I am very grateful as well.

About the Author

Lacole Smith hails from the small town of Ethel, Louisiana. A healthcare professional by day, author by night. She believes God spared her life so she could tell her story, and she uses it to inspire and empower all who cross her path.

Lacole Smith is the beautiful wife of Shedric Smith, loving daughter of Rev. Howard Young and the Late Rev. Mother Audrey V. Young, older sister of twin siblings Miriam and Moses Young (Marquitta Young), and the mother of 4 wonderful young ladies Daneqa A. Dunn (Brandon Dunn), ShaQuea Schiele, LaQuea Schiele, and Indea Schiele and has 6 beautiful grandkids - Jayden, Alyssa, Princeton, Rylan, Noah, and Raiden.

She is the Creator and Founder of Motivational Talk where she is also the Co-Panelist of MT Ladies Night Show. She is also the CEO of Motivational Talk Dialogues Show where she interviews upcoming/established authors and others who are making a difference in the community. She is the Co-Founder of a non-profit, Anointed Sisters United (ASU). Lacole is also the Owner of Godsent Fashions and Godsent Vacations. Lacole is an author whose book and journal will come out late November 2022. She is a Motivational Speaker that loves helping others change their lives.

When she is not writing , Lacole spends most of her time with her family, reading, cooking, traveling, and catching her favorite television shows. She's an adamant football fan who shares her love of the game with her husband and in-house rival.

Learn more about Lacole Smith by visiting her website:

AuthorLacoleSmith.com

Or contact her via the following:

Email: **AuthorLacoleSmith@gmail.com**

Facebook: **Author Lacole Smith**

Instagram: **@authorlacolesmith**

Made in the USA
Columbia, SC
13 April 2024

34172075R00065